THEN AND NOW

POEMS AND PRAYERS FROM A LIFETIME

by

Mary Ann Stafford, EdD

authorHOUSE®

AuthorHouse™
1663 Liberty Drive, Suite 200
Bloomington, IN 47403
www.authorhouse.com
Phone: 1-800-839-8640

© *2007 Mary Ann Stafford, EdD. All rights reserved.*

No part of this book may be reproduced, stored in a retrieval system, or transmitted by any means without the written permission of the author.

First published by AuthorHouse 12/4/2007

ISBN: 978-1-4343-4700-8 (sc)

Library of Congress Control Number: 2007908449

Printed in the United States of America
Bloomington, Indiana

This book is printed on acid-free paper.

TO THE READER:

I am an artist. I paint in pastels and water media. I have done this all my life, and I can't imagine a time when I wasn't involved in some sort of visual art. It is who I am. Because of this, you will find many poems and prayers in this volume that hint at an artist's sensibilities. I have lived a long time; had many children and grandchildren; seen a lot of agony, suffering, and joy. I praise and thank God every day for my life and for those who are in my life – my husband of 55 years, my eight children, and my 25 grandchildren and two great-grandchildren. I have been blessed beyond measure. If any of these humble writings of mine reach your heart, I am most grateful.

You will also note that most of these works are spiritual in nature. I am not apologizing for this, because this is where my inspiration comes from. I have questioned, sought, and prayed for faith most of my life, and faith has come to me through the grace of God. It is natural that this faith is manifested in my personal writings. And these writings are very personal.

I write sporadically, I'm afraid. For a time, I wrote in a journal every morning, but now I do this only when something begs for me to write it down. That's the way most of my poems occur – at night, when I am hovering between waking and sleep, and in quiet times after reading scripture or a spiritual writing. The poems come to me already formed; I just have to polish them a little.

At any rate, this is my little book that I want to share with you. I have included a few black and white images of some of my paintings as well as the color image on the front cover. You can see more of my art on my website, www.staffordart.com.

I had a problem deciding how to organize my poems. There are certain themes, such as family, despair, aging, etc., but some of these themes overlap others. I finally decided to keep it simple – to organize them chronologically to go along with my title. So those I wrote at an earlier time when I was a teacher and mother can be found in front; those written later will be in the back. You will note that the earlier poems are mostly about teaching and raising a family; some of these are quite painful. The later ones seem to be more about questioning, searching, and finding. A lot of my poems have to do with aging and anticipation of death. Considering the direction that life is taking me now, there will probably be other poems popping into my mind in the future. If so, I'll let you know.

Contents

III. GROWING OLDER

ILLUSTRATIONS

Cover – *The Perfect Tree* – mixed media

GROWING A
FAMILY

To My Valentine, My Husband

If I forget to say, "I love you,"
A thousand times each day,
It's because I get so wrapped up
In cares along the way.

If I don't say: "Thank you, thank you,"
And hug and kiss you too,
It's because I get so busy
With the things I have to do.

But still, you are my hero,
And I'm so glad you're mine.
There can never be another
Cause you're my only Valentine.

To My Husband

You've given me
eight healthy children.
(More than enough
to prove your love.)
I love each of them
for that special something
That sets them apart
from other men's
children.
But dear, don't ever think
I don't love you as much.

I love you more.

September Song

He's so happy about his new adventure
His new friends, the new things he's learning
He can't wait to get to go to school
In the first grade.

Soon he starts making excuses: his head hurts,
He has a stomach ache.
He begs to stay home from school
In the third grade.

He loses interest and brings home mediocre grades.
He complains about too much homework.
He gets his first F. He cuts his first class
In the sixth grade.

He stops paying attention in class and never
Turns in an assignment, He seems to be
Interested only in football and girls
In the eighth grade.

A teacher cuts him down in front of the class
And a kid laughs. Later, he hits the kid
On the school grounds and is suspended
In the tenth grade.

He seldom goes to school and starts
Running with the wrong crowd. He misses
Too many days of school and drops out
In the eleventh grade.

Now he stands on the street corner.
Can't find a job and couldn't keep one if he did.
He talks about a GED, but we both know
he doesn't have the will.

(con't.)

What ever happened to that bright-eyed,
Excited little boy of six who skipped rather
Than walked to school that first September day?
Why did the joy of learning burn out so soon?

If we knew, could we stop it from happening again?

The Shape Of Things To Come

New curls and new clothes,
Jeans, baggy sweaters and panty hose
Secret phone calls and knowing looks
Notes from boys stuck in her books.
What next? a bra, size AAA cup.
My little girl is growing up.

Disciplinary Action

The little boy in the six-foot frame leans against the door,
His ball cap tipped rakishly on his head,
Self-confidence exuding from every pore
And a silly smirk on his beardless face.

He thinks I don't know
That underneath it all—
He's scared to death!

Late Night Ruminations

It's not that I don't like you.
I've never had a student I didn't like, or love, for that matter.
It's not that I don't understand you—I realize you have problems:
Your folks won't listen to you and only expect the worst from you.
They don't trust you, even though you're seventeen now.
And it's not that I don't empathize with you—
God knows I've been through it all myself.

But why do you demand so much of me?
The constant questioning, the pleading for approval,
The distractions that clutter up my well-swept mind.
Why don't you just leave me alone and let me teach?
That's what I get paid for. Sit in your nice, rigid little row
And let me fertilize your undeveloped brain.
That's what education is all about, isn't it? Or is it?
Let's look at this another way.

What if you never caught me in a mistake?
Never questioned a method or spoke out about a possible injustice?
But sat quietly at your desk and did all I asked,
Like a mindless puppet who spoke only when I pulled your ring.
Every day like any other – every student like any other.
Nameless, faceless, emotionless.
Who could exist in such a sterile desert? Who would grow?
Who would be your mentor? Your role model?

Who would counteract the garbage you see and hear
On TV, in the movies, in songs each day?
Who would strengthen your values, your sense of fair play?
And what about me? Would I start each day with a smile
Eager for whatever challenges the day would bring? I think not.
So bring on your questions, your yearnings, your uncertainties.
Help me remember that teaching is more than imparting knowledge.
Help me remember why I'm here.

The Change-about Artist

Whoever said, "Clothes don't make the man,"
has never seen my son
Erupting from ragged jeans and grimy shirt
to Sunday best on the run.

He splashes water outside the tub
and comes out dripping wet
With hair all matted down in front
like a farmhand's thick with sweat.

He fights his brother for the new green shirt
and comes out for once the winner.
He struggles with last year's pants
for which he should be slimmer.

When he's all dressed and I have
finally combed his shining hair
And polished his shoes and fixed his tie
and zipped his fly to there,

He looks at me with his sheepish grin,
and not a girl among you
Could argue with me when I say,
"He's a right handsome youngun."

Grieving Over A Lost Child

You are not dead, I know,
Although sometimes I think that might be easier
Then I wouldn't have this false hope
That someday the phone would ring
And I'd hear your voice on the line.

I carried you in my womb for nine months,
Bathed you, fed you, diapered you,
Treated your hurts, comforted your pain,
Gave you advice, dried your tears
And drove you where you needed to go.

I washed your clothes, paid your bills,
Watched your ball games,
Met with your teachers,
Listened to your woes,
And even got you out of jail one time.

How many sleepless nights did I worry
About you, dreading the late night phone call
That meant you were in trouble again?
But always giving you the second chance
Because my love was great.

But yet, you've turned your back on me.
Forgotten the one who gave you life.
At times, I'm angry; at others, perplexed
If only I knew what caused your pain
And could change what I did wrong.

Rude Awakening

Our shells encase us
Envelop us
Entrap us
Protect us from the beyond.

What gentle tapping awakens us?
How dare you shatter our safety
And expose our pulsating inner selves
To the light?

Christ In The Window

I walked by a large plate glass window
And automatically looked therein.
Reflected there was a homeless man
Resting against the lamppost.
His tattered garment was held close;
His loneliness like a shield against the wind.

In the next block, a child was playing with a ball.
He chased it laughing as it rolled up against the
Building and stopped.
He ran to it and deftly scooped it up.
As I gazed at his reflection in the restaurant door,
I saw the fun and excitement of youth.

Farther on, I saw a young mother shepherding three
Small children; one in her arms and two at her side.
Her concern for her children was mirrored in her face
As she gently guided her girls toward home.
Her image in the shop window
Reflected a mother's love and protection.

I thought of Jesus, and realized that I saw Him
In each of these three faces today.
In the reflected loneliness, happiness, and concern.
As I entered my home, I glanced at my reflection
In the hall mirror. To my surprise, I saw not my face
But His.

Panic Button

Breathe in, breathe out.
Don't cry, don't shout.
Take it easy, settle down.
Keep it simple, lose the frown.

Pause a while, sit a spell.
Stop the circus; stop it well.
Dream a little, pray a lot.
Thank the Lord for what you've got.

Things could be much worse, you know.
It's bound to help if you take it slow.
Forget your woes, say a prayer.
Fretting won*t get you anywhere.

If you for once jump off the merry-go-round
What's most important in life can be found.
Stress and worry soon will cease,
For deep within is God's own peace.

Quiet My Life

REFRAIN: Turn down the volume of the world, O Lord.
Quiet my life, I pray.
I cannot hear your small, still voice
When my daily cares are in the way.

God speaks to man in a small, whispering sound,
Not in the roaring thunder's boom.
Be still, my soul, that I might hear;
Be calm, my life, that I might know.

Sirens wailing, babies crying,
Loud pop music in my ear.
Phones are ringing, horns are blaring,
The noises of life are everywhere.

From time to time I realize
That on the path I trod,
Round and round, the faster I go,
The farther I travel from my God.

Then it's time to stop and pray awhile,
And look for the inner peace I need
That when my call comes from the Lord
I will hear his voice and will heed.

Wake Up!

Wake up! It's time to come out and play!

The birds are chirping in the elm trees.
The breeze is blowing sweetly upon my face.
The scent of lilacs floats on the wind,
And I am wanting to jump and romp,
To play hide and seek with a squirrel,
To wade barefoot through that puddle of mud,
And climb that maple tree that beckons
In the neighbor's back yard.

Wake up! It's time to come out and play!

The Role Model

You say that I'm your role model--
Please don't put that burden on me.
You have no idea of the sins I've sinned,
The awful mistakes I've made,
The promises I've failed to keep.
And heavens knows, I'm not finished yet.
I wouldn't want to fail you
The way I've failed myself.

Instead, look to the perfect role model
You know His story, you've read His words.
He walked the earth as a man--
A man in all our weaknesses and temptations
But in truth, He was divine.
And He taught us how to live.
He'll speak to you if you'll let Him,
And He'll guide your way better than I.

Because a role model knows where she's going;
She doesn't make stupid mistakes.
She's sure-footed, confident, and strong--
Not one who stumbles and falls
And misses the right turns
And takes detours that go absolutely nowhere.
Besides, I'm on the same journey as you
And may even be lagging a little behind you.

GROWING IN
MATURITY

New Year's Day

A new beginning, another chance
To begin again, to make a new start
More blessed time to do what I can
To change my life and change my heart

A time for mercy, a time for healing
A time to practice justice and peace
A time to give my life to Him
A time to see my worries cease.

The grass needs not my concern;
It comes up every year on its own
Plant the crocuses once in fall
And lo, in March, flowers are grown.

In this New Year, I resolve to be
A better neighbor, mother, and wife,
A listener, a helper, and a guide--
A comfort to those who share my life.

Within The Spaces

I live in the spaces between:

Between the downs and ups—
Between the valleys and mountains,
Between the ugliness and the beauty,
Between the losses and the wins.

Between the grief and the joy,
Between the desperation and the hope,
Between the meanness and the love,
Between the beginnings and the ends.

Between the apathy and the care,
Between the doubt and my faith,
Between the pain and the well-being,
Between the wrong and the right.

Between the dusk and the dawn,
Between the confusion and the clear,
Between the problems and the solutions,
Between the storm and the sunlight.

Between dreaming and waking,
Between the questions and the answers,
Between the now and then,
Between the sorrow and delight.

For God is in the spaces, too.
Look for Him there, please do.

Gifts

A reed in a windstorm,
I think myself strong and graceful.
A sudden gust whips me around
And snaps off my tallest spike.
I ask, "What would you have me
Learn from this, O Lord?"
He answers: "Humility."

A pebble on the bank of a still pond,
I expect to spend my days in quiet rest.
A ripple dislodges me and moves me
To a crowded place in a flowing stream.
I ask, "What would you have me
Learn from this, O Lord?"
He answers: "Obedience."

A seed sprouting in the warm earth,
I imagine how tall and mighty I'll be.
Many years pass by and still
I yearn to reach my destined height.
I ask, "What would you have me
Learn from this, O Lord?"
He answers: "Patience."

A cherry tree in the prime of life,
I delight in the rich red fruits I produce.
Birds come and eat my choicest fruit
And leave the rest to rot.
I ask, "What would you have me
Learn from this, O Lord?"
He answers: "Love."

(con't.)

A chrysalis glistening in the sun
I snuggle in the cool darkness of my world.
An inner force suddenly expels me
And I flutter hesitantly in the light.
I ask, "What would you have me
Learn from this, O Lord?"
He answers: "Salvation."

The Puzzle

There they lie, all 1500.
Painstakingly turned up so that
I can see them all at one time.

I have put the borders together
So all that is now required
Is to fit the pieces into their spaces.

A kaleidoscope of shapes, colors, patterns--
Too much to fit together correctly
Without the help of the picture before me.

This image is my guide to help me
Find the right shape for the right space.
In two weeks, perhaps I'll be done.

The tiger will be seen in all his glory,
Each color and shape perfectly aligned
To put him in his forest environment.

But now, it's all a jumble;
A disarray in bits and pieces--
Unfocused, disjointed, like my life.

I have no image to guide me
In putting together the whole picture--
The design of my life

But you, O Lord, know me well.
You guide me, even though I'm unaware.
Blindly, I trust in your mercy.

My final design; my part of your plan,
Is not for me know in advance.
The final solution is in the end.

Hope Eternal

Humans wage war against their own;
Kill and maim with weapons extreme;
Threaten, invade, plunder, and rob --
But still, the dormant grass grows green.

Power and greed consume the most.
Politicians evade, distort, and lie.
Not one cares for the least of all --
But still, the red-breasted robins thrive.

The homeless, jobless, depressed, and ill
Deprived of love and one to care
Learn first-hand of the evil of men --
But still, the dogwood flourishes there.

The birds build nests in the old oak tree.
Spring rains cleanse away the winter's grime.
Tulips and irises pop up from the soil --
And hope, like Easter, arrives on time.

Oncoming Winter

Leaves and pine cones all over the lawn.
A nip in the air that serves to warn
Winter is on its way.

Colors are changing: red, gold, and brown
The wind through the trees makes a rustling sound.
Nature is fashioning a glorious day.

I welcome the cold air, the snow, the short day,
The slant of the sun as it moves away.
I do not mourn the loss of warm.

Winter is needed for us to know
That rest is essential for all to grow,
And even death has its charm.

My Father

He was not really a father to me
Like those you see
In old TV movies.
He did not play games with me,
Talk to me,
Read me stories.
I can't ever remember his hugging me
Or telling me that he loved me.
He was just there.

He was a good man.
He provided for his family.
He was kind and gentle,
Fun-loving and generous.
I know this because
He had many friends
Who loved him.
I might have loved him
Had I known him.

I cannot judge him.
He was a product of his time,
As we are all products of the times
In which we live.
I forgive him as I hope my children
Will forgive me.
Life is a cycle of mistakes
From which succeeding generations
Reap a harvest of pain and joy.

We learn from both,
But sometimes,
We learn too late.

Clay Pots

An earthenware vessel am I,
Not from stoneware or porcelain made.
Formed from the clay of the earth
As was Adam in times long ago.

Clay fashioned by God's tender hands
And tested in the fire of existence.
Broken perhaps, imperfect for sure,
But useful in ways I never can know.

Stoneware is purer and stronger than clay,
And porcelain is more refined,
Decorative and lovely, set on a shelf,
Lovely vessels to use and to show.

But I am simple and crude.
The commonest of containers, it's true.
But filled with the love of the Lord,
His fruits within me will grow.

Early Morning

There's something about waking up at 4:00 a.m.
That causes the imagination to flow.
The rational mind may still be asleep, but
The other is free to go.

Why can't someone invent a machine
That records our ideas when half awake
So we remember the thoughts we just had?
Think what great poems I could make!

Wounds May Heal, But Scars Remain

Eyes wide open at 4:00 a.m.,
My mind recalls the words my lips cannot:
Those unbidden, unwanted words that cut and ripped at our love.

If time, like memory, could crawl backwards
And erase the harm that was done,
How much better than saying, "I'm sorry."

Like the skin repairs itself after trauma,
Re-knitting and closing in on itself,
We can repair damage to the heart, too.

But only so far.
Wounds may heal, but scars remain.

A Consideration Of Time

I don't waste time—
I mangle it, crush it, stomp on it,
Wring it dry.

If I could, I'd turn it
Inside out on itself so that all my yesterdays
Would be tomorrows again.

I'd rip its seams
From stem to stern and sew it back again
Into a new configuration.

But as it is,
I can only squeeze it like a tube of toothpaste
So that all the fullness is at the top

Ready to pop out
And bring the freshness of each morning into
My eager mouth.

A Prayer Of Despair

Great God--the vastness of space--
The innumerable stars, galaxies,
And universes you have created;

The limitless life forms; the simple and complex
Organisms here on this small planet;
Who can count them all?

Who can possible imagine the complexities
Of infinity? You made it all.

You set man and woman into this world so fair.
You set them as rulers over all your creations
The masters of this universe.

What marvelous things have we accomplished with your gifts?
Greed, violence, idolatry,
Senseless killings and brutality,

Wars - both hot and cold,
Petty jealousies, racial and ethnic hatred,
Obsessions with the sensational,
Poverty, famine, disease.

O Lord, my God!
When will you give up on us
And pull the plug?

Simple Joys

Lying down at night on a bed with clean sheets,
Feeling the breeze through my hair on a hot summer evening,
My cat lying quietly by my side as I cross stitch,
A good book just waiting to be started on my night table,

My grandchild's laughter as he tells me a joke,
And his bright eyes and wide grin when first he sees me,
A bubble-bath in a deep tub of almost hot water,
A fragrant candle and cup of hot chocolate sitting close by,

Dark purple clouds heralding a summer storm,
Jagged strokes of lightning cutting across the shaded skies,
The sound of thunder rumbling overhead,
And suddenly, shafts of sunlight peeking through the clouds,

An icy cold beer in a frosty mug,
Celebrating family get-togethers at the local restaurant,
Early morning prayer on my porch swing
While red and yellow flowers raise their heads to the sun,

Visiting with neighbors in the front yard,
Seeing movies, shows, plays, and dances with friends,
Taking part in our Sunday liturgies,
Receiving my Lord in the guise of bread and wine.

For all these things, I thank you, Lord.

Regret

Alone. Imprisoned in the nursing home,
Crippled and frail, she remembers the past.
What happened to her young girl dreams?
The dreams of becoming an artist--
Sharing with others the joy she felt?

Instead, she married the boy next door
Because it was expected.
She had many handsome, healthy children,
And made a good home for her family.
That too was expected.

Now she regrets the children of her soul;
The paintings she should have borne,
The poems she should have penned.
She wonders, now that it's all too late,
"What about my expectations?"

Sonnet To A Friend On Her 40th Birthday

You are fast approaching with smiles and gay laughter
The delicate age at which "life begins after..."
With loving, affectionate children gathered round you,
Serenity, love, and contentment have found you.
No major decisions as to what you should wear,
What boy you should date, what's best for your hair—
The right thing to do—parents' moral ruling,
The fire's not quite out, but it seems to be cooling!
No fighting the pimples, the establishment, the pill,
No staying out late, no dancing until—
No upsetting love life – someone different each day.
The old man's no lover, but at least he will stay.
So face the oncoming years with a grin.
Wouldn't you really hate to be a teenager again?

Suffering

In the midst of crisis,
O God, hear our cry.
When we don't understand
And cannot reason why.

Is there no answer, Lord?
Why can't you make things right?
It seems you're always hidden
And silent in the night.

When we hurt too much to pray
And wander senselessly in the dark,
We trust your living mercy
Will enfold us like a cloak.

You never promised us
A life devoid of pain,
But promised always to be there
As our support again and again.

When our lives are over
And we stand before the judge
Our eyes will then be opened,
And we'll know how much we're loved.

Retired

When I was a young and dutiful wife
With a large family already begun
I never considered my future life
Or even if I'd have one.
My only thoughts were of how I could try
To feed my burgeoning brood,
And where I would get the dough to buy
Cheap, yet nourishing food.

But I placed my trust in Jesus and Yes,
He was always there for me.
Our marriage seemed to be blessed.
I was fulfilling my destiny.
And now our children are grown and gone
To live their own special ways.
My trust in my Lord is still strong,
My days spent in endless praise.

Psalm 12

For honest men and women,
The kindness they show each day.
For the love they feel for every human being
As they walk along Christ's way.
For their humble trust and faith in God's promise
The spirit within them as they pray,
O Lord, I give thanks and praise.

For the sun that warms my skin,
The breeze that cools my brow,
The animals that scamper across my path,
The freshness of a summer shower,
For the shapes and smells of morning,
For the life that beats within me now
O Lord, I give thanks and praise.

The Guises Of Grief

Grief comes in many forms:
Stoically as a tall shrouded stranger
Withdrawn within himself
No tears, no outcries.

To some, he comes violently--
Screaming, tearing of clothes,
Falling down and heart-rending,
Like a frenzied dervish.

And then again, he seems to hide--
Creeping out gradually like a stalking tiger
And finally pouncing on its victim,
Who thought that grief had been vanquished.

The only way to handle grief
And keep your sanity,
Is to embrace him – hold him dear
Learn how to live with him.

Someday, he might take a holiday
And give you a chance to bask in the sun--
To feel whole again before returning to his
Usual place in your heart.

Year after year his days off
Will lengthen and come more often,
Even though he always returns
On birthdays, anniversaries, holidays.

But then, you know,
You will never be fully rid of him.

Simple Gifts

The simple gifts are the best:
Family, Nature, Language,
Not only verbal, but those other languages:
Music, dance, poetry, and art
Which touch our hearts and minds.
Wisdom, the holy wisdom of men and women of all ages
Coming together in Christ.
And above all, the gift of the Holy Spirit, which
Although not simple, is there for us all.

Ode To Newness

Ah, the joy of New things!
The glistening dew on grass in the morn;
The wrinkled, red face of a babe just born;
The pristine white of a watercolor sheet
Just before a brilliant wash of color it meets;
A new recipe, a new menu to try;
A summer shower on soil parched dry;
A pair of new shoes and a purse to match;
Baby birds in a nest just starting to hatch;
The first crocus that heralds arrival of spring;
And the budding of trees that we know it will bring;
The start of school or change of career;
A new day, a new week, and a happy New Year;
A white t-shirt without stains or tears;
But best of all, a new someone who cares.

A Good Model In Her Day

My old Cadillac's definitely past her prime.
The odometer's turned over one last time.

The gas tank's a guzzler; I buy gas each hour.
The alternator's shot, and now I'm losing power.

But when all's said and done, I haven't a care,
Cause the ride is so smooth, I'm floating on air.

I don't even realize it when I am speeding:
It's such a shock to see 70 on the reading!

It still looks great, and I can truthfully say
She was a very good model in her day.

I guess my body's about the same way.
I've got more wrinkles, and my hair's turning gray.

I exercise, watch my weight and cholesterol measure,
Get check-ups for diseases, sneezes, and high blood pressure.

And I can still do all the things I used to--
Just can't do them as fast as I'd choose to.

And life's a lot easier now that my mistakes are all made.
For the life of a teenager, I surely wouldn't trade.

The Awakening

My heart was closed; I knew not why.
I could not love; my life was dry.
I prayed for faith my doubts to sway
And one by one, they fell away.

You spoke to me; I fought Your call
You spoke again; I gave my all.
I learned to care; I learned to share
I learned that love dwelt everywhere.

I opened up and in You came.
You filled my life: I'm not the same.
And now it seems my only quest
Is to be with You eternally blest.

GROWING OLDER

The Vagrant

Where did you go, old friend?
I've looked for you everywhere,
But you just keep slipping away from me.
I see someone I've known for years
And can't think of her name.

I try to speak, and find that words
Elude me; words I had a strong command
Of a few sentences ago.
It tends to be most embarrassing
And difficult to cover up.

Am I getting that dread disease
The scourge of the elderly?
Come back to me, dear friend
Don't play games with me.
This is serious stuff.

Make It Count

Make it count.
We're only here for an instant.
Make it count.

The world is passing.
Eternity lasts.
Make it count.

From apathy to awareness,
From sympathy to love,
Make it count.

What else matters?
The important thing is love.
Make it count.

Love for ourselves, love for others,
Above all, love for our Lord.
That is what counts.

Make it count.

I Give Thanks

For giving me life – for a heritage of proud German inventiveness and stout sturdy health.

For this bounteous globe on which we live – the air we breathe – the joy of seasons that vary and save us from boredom.

For the form and color of plants and flowers – the miracle of growth – of watching seeds sprout and form leaves to bring either sustenance, beauty, or both.

For the companionship of a spouse who stays with me through sickness and health, poverty and prosperity.

For children, grandchildren, and yes, even great grandchildren – to see the future in their eyes and in their strength of character.

To know that even though the sun doesn't always shine – and gray days may outnumber the bright – that my God is always with me and He loves me.

And that when I die – I will be with him forever. I thank you, Lord. Amen.

An Artist's Realization

Brat that I am,
I think God will answer all my requests
In the manner I want.

I forget sometimes
That even though the Almighty
Loves me and wants to please me,

He is the Almighty
And he knows what's best
What's best for not just me,

But everyone around me.
He sees the whole picture,
While we only see one section of the grid.

For life is not a puzzle—
It's a master work of art
Built on a grid of infinite dimension.

Only One can step back and see
How the work is progressing,
And what else needs to be done.

And we, with our narrow point of view
Can only see one small section at a time
In very limited perspective.

Just that small section itself
Can sometimes be vague in neutral tones
Or clear and hard-edged.

But if we could see the whole work,
We'd understand our place in it.
And how our particular patterns affect the whole.

Forgive our impatience, Lord,
And refine the brushstrokes of our lives.
Keep us in your master picture.

Morning Prayer

My God, my Maker, my Creator—
You built me from my very start.
You gifted me with countless blessings;
Give me now a loving heart.

I want to see the pain and grief
In others who need my care.
And having seen Your Face in them,
With courage, I can be there.

Many years in the past, I know
I have not done your will.
But now, I pray to be your tool,
Your plan for me fulfill.

Take this humble heart of mine
And fill it with your grace
Until it overflows with love
And leaves of self no trace.

Basic Shapes

Simplify. Go back to Square One.
Reduce to basic shapes.

Look for the essential,
All encompassing truth.

What else matters
In the overall scheme of things?

Draw one line across a sheet of paper—
Behold—a landscape.

Two lines meeting at a slant
Connected at the base by a third,

Become a pyramid, a steeple,
Praying hands.

A vertical intersecting a horizontal
An axis, a telephone pole, or a cross --

Enclose a circle however misshapen
A moon, a sun, a baby's face.

The simplest truth of all is this:
To know that we are loved.

The Dark Side Of Families

A black hole that I try not to think about
Insinuates itself into my consciousness from time to time.
If I let it—it will eat up my contentment--
The false sense of a close, ordinary family.

Something in the past I think,
Something better left hidden and forgotten,
Could shatter my very existence
If I let it be known.

Is it like this in other families?
Do other mothers hide their fears behind
Shiny facades of pleasantries
And never acknowledge the darkness?

Should one face reality and
Run the risk of destroying a fragile unity?
Does the truth really set one free,
Or only alone?

Read The Scriptures

Read, read the Scriptures
If you want to know God.
Put yourself in God's hands
And turn everything over to Him.
Not just your problems,
Although He takes on that burden, too,
But your very life—your will.
Submit, give in, open up—
Welcome, accept, trust.

Only then can you begin to grow.
Only then will you become fully
A partner, a brother with Him who loves you.
The rewards are beyond comprehension.
Fortunate are those allowed a long life
Who do not die at an early age.
Given time to deepen their faith,
Their spiritual journey will take them further
Into a communion of love.

Father Abraham

Abraham, Father of Faith,
Bring all your children together.
Hebrew, Christian, and Muslim.
Teach them to see their oneness,
Not their divisions.

Show them how to live
According to their teachings:
David, Jesus, Mohammed.
The root of all three faiths
Began in the desert with you.

If there is but one God,
He is God of all; there is no other.
His truths encompass all religions.
Humans pervert the sacred scriptures
And reverse the meanings at will.

To you great father Abraham,
Patriarch of all Bible and Koran
I present this plea,
Return to us and set us straight
Before it is too late.

Jesus, I Love You (Hymn)

In desert lands I wander
Always looking for a home.
You are there to guide me
And I find I'm not alone.

REFRAIN:
Jesus, I love you.
Jesus, I trust you.
Jesus I need you
Close to me now.

You fashion and mold me
Though sometimes through pain.
In good times and bad times
I will call out your name.

REFRAIN

Jesus, I love you.
Jesus, I trust you.
Jesus I need you
Close to me now.

And now that I'm aged,
Growing feeble and lame
Through sickness and sorrow,
Your love's still the same.

REFRAIN

Jesus, I love you.
Jesus, I trust you
Jesus, I feel you
Close to me now.

The Grand Design

Like a silver thread just waiting to be cut,
Our lives hang between life and death.
Not able to read the whole pattern,
Not able to see the tapestry,
We have no inkling of the day or time.

We wonder if the garment is complete
Or if there is more to our design.
Our trust is in the designer's eye
Who visualizes the masterworks of ages.
Our faith transcends our narrow vision

And rejoices in the harmony of life.

The Demise Of Doubt

Where do I find You, O Lord?
Am I blind that I cannot see?
Deaf that I cannot hear?
Reveal Your mighty presence to me.

I see You in the shafts of sunlight
Reflecting in bands across the plains.
I smell You in the honeysuckle
Perfuming my walks on country lanes.

I hear You in the rustle of water over rocks
And see Your artistry in the sunrise hues
Above the distant mountains
You're painting with purples, pinks, & blues.

The laughter of children as they play,
The singing of birds on a morn in June,
The simple song of a gifted musician,
And the glorious harmony of choirs in tune.

I hear You in a mother's soft croon,
As she quiets her tiny baby's cry.
I see you in the hands of the priest
As he raises bread and wine on high.
.
I see You in the elderly couple who sit in the pew
Holding hands during daily Mass.
I see you in the eyes of those who suffer,
And who know that this too, will pass.

I feel you in the gathering of those who serve you—
Who have dedicated their lives to those in need.
In the gift of food and shelter
To the hungry and homeless they feed.

I see You in the young men and women, teens and adults
Who learn to minister while in their prime.
I see You in the throng of children dressed in white
Receiving your body and blood for the first time

No less ourselves are we part of the proof
With our efficiently functioning body and mind
And the spirit that searches, searches
For a close union with the Creator to bind.

I feel You in the quiet of my home
Where I read your words so clear.
I hear You when you speak to me
And I fall on my knees in prayer.

My Sister

For fifty years, my oldest sister annoyed me.
In younger days, she told me how to live my life,
How to raise my kids, clean my house
In short, trying to be (in her eyes) my mother.

As we both aged, she interrupted me,
Focused on herself, spoke of her own problems,
Matters I certainly wasn't interested in,
And other irritating quirks.

Then older, she copied my hair styles, my clothes,
What I bought and what I said,
And told others my inmost secrets,
Things I told her in confidence.

But now that she's gone, these things seem unimportant.
What I remember now is her desire to please me—
The gifts she gave me, her willingness to go anywhere anytime,
Her love of shopping, of cooking, of playing cards.

She loved life, and at the end, she wanted to stay.
Soon, however, she gave it up and accepted
The inevitability of death.
And this is what I remember most now--

Her courage, her faith, and her love.
All else is fading like a shade drawn on the past.
What remains now are only her virtues.
A legacy that all could envy.

I Believe In Jesus (Hymn)

Refrain:I believe in Christ Jesus
I believe in His promise.
I believe He will show me Heaven
And I believe I'll soon be there.

So many times I've doubted
And questioned all in vain
But then the Holy Spirit
Revived my soul again.

When doubts and fears assail me
From places I know not where,
I call out the name of my savior
And He always answers my prayer.

Though many trials and sorrows
My God has seen me through,
He comforts me and strengthens--
He'll do the same for you.

In the midst of pain and suffering
When I'm bowed low by care,
I remember the One who is listening
The One who will always be there.

He goes to prepare a place for us,
This is what He said.
He is the way if we'd just follow
The path on which we're led.

I know now the secret
Of giving myself to Him.
My trust has grown; my heart is full,
My life an endless hymn.

My Gift

My life is a gift to you, O Lord.
A package tied up with bright curly ribbons
And wrapped with the brown paper of everyday life.

If you open it, you'll see
All my hopes, disillusionments, weaknesses,
Petty complaints, and jealousies.

But you'll also see a lifetime of love
And service to you, O Lord.
Will it be enough? Does it please you?

What more can I do?

The Unlit Candle

God gives us each a candle to light--
Our life, as it shines, to brighten the night.
What a marvelous gift to share with the world
If only we*d light it, and live by His Word.

Eager and willing to make a great name,
I rushed through my youth to keep mine aflame.
When faced with setbacks that I could not mend,
My candle went out with a gust of the wind.

Many a year went by in the dark.
My candle forgotten, a stone in my heart.
Unloved, unforgiving, alone among men,
One day I discovered the candle unspent.

My life has gone by and soon it will end.
I have no one to love, not even a friend.
Too soon I gave up, too soon I quit
And all because of the candle not lit.

(Written with my husband, Lyle)

Proof

A few moments of peace with you, Lord --
Let me sit quietly in your presence.

So much life abounds--
Hidden, pulsating life,

Molecules moving rapidly--
The visible life.

Squirrels, birds, my cat,
Trucks on the highway behind my house,

Neighbors backing out of their driveways,
Garbage cans being towed out to the curbs.

Friends waving to friends,
Flower buds opening on their tall stems,

New green shoots on shrubs,
Tomatoes turning pink in the garden.

All around me, proof of your existence, O Lord,
And your unconditional love.

You Don't Know Me

You don't know me.
You don't know how I cry at night
Because my babies have grown up
And moved away.

You don't know what brings me joy--
What makes my heart sing,
Or my eyes swell with
Tears of happiness.

You don't know how I feel inside
When I realize that God has sent me
Another opportunity to
Grow and to praise.

And you don't know my fears--
My fears of not being good enough,
Or strong enough to bear the
Trials that lie ahead.

For the end of my life is
Approaching, and I long
For someone who understands-
For someone who knows me.

Aging Gracefully

On each side of my mouth are some not-so-fine lines
That can't be smoothed with a smile.
In my legs there's a stiffness I find every time
I walk after sitting a while.

My memory has not been the same,
I grope for words I once knew.
My hair has become coarse and untamed
Dark strands, not even a few.

The skin on my arms like old parchment,
Translucent, wrinkled, and thin.
The slightest jar to my arms or my legs
Leaves bruises again and again.

But I'm still the same person down deep inside
That for many long years I have been.
I still want to dance, to play in the sun
To do what I did way back when

When I was young, and pretty, and slim
And felt healthy and strong ever still.
When my blood pressure always was low
And not regulated daily by pill.

How sad to grow old and change for the worse
At least, that's what some people would say
But I still wouldn't trade all the youth in the world
For the journey I've had on the way.

Prayer For Death

I have one wish of which I speak.
Death be gentle, Death be quick.

Pray do not choose to take your time
To end this bitter life of mine.

I do not wish to linger on
With loss of mind and weak of bone.

It seems to me a bit less cruel
If the master switch at once you'd pull

And do not saunter to and fro
Dimming the lights where ere you go.

Best for me, your new found friend,
If you make of me a sudden end.

In God's good grace, I ask this boon.
Let me depart this life and soon.

Look Within

We are all a part of God
The Divine is within us.
Don't stifle it.

Look deep within yourself
To find the Divine.
It is not hard to do.

Life is unpredictable,
And we are all connected
To every living thing.

Once you've found your own divinity
Look outward to others,
To the land, the sky, the animals, the plants.

No less is the Divine there also.

For Noah

A baby boy, four months old
Sleeps in his silky white bed.
His "binky" clutched in his little hand,
His Pooh bears arranged at his head.

His Momma and others who loved him so
Are amazed to see him there.
They know his perfect, pure soul
Has left to play with angels somewhere.

Noah, her darling baby, has passed away.
His stillness is wrong somehow.
He will not wake when she calls his name,
He sleeps with the angels now.

The angels are happy he's joined them.
They love to hear him laugh and play.
But oh, how lonesome his Momma now
That little Noah has gone away.

(on the loss of my first great grand-child)

Circles

Grief has a way of bringing us all together in a circle.
The circle begins at birth.
A baby touches those around him,
Draws others to himself.
Who can resist a cuddly, vulnerable little creature who needs so much?

From there, the circle spreads outward.
Women especially are drawn into the circle.
From mother to grandmother, to great grandmother,
The concentric circles expand.
But the circles spiral even further to include other family, other friends.

Countless are the hearts that are touched by one little soul.
When that soul dies, the circle retracts – closes in on the mother now
As the center of love.
She is surrounded, as if the shelter of love will protect
Her from the pain of loss.

This gets her through the funeral.
But eventually, the mother must come to grips with reality.
The support circle moves back allowing
The mother to grow and change.
Death is never an end, but it is a beginning.

Quietly and gradually, the circles change.
The mother begins to form new circles –
New activities, new friends—
The old circles are still there, but
Overlapped by the newer ones.

(con't.)

Some are not strong, and they die quickly.
Some others become like steel rings that must be broken
Because they are too confining.
But one or two become the circles that empower and support
Contracting and expanding when needed,

Like the original circles of baby, mother,
Grandmother, and Great Grandmother.
Nothing is ever wasted in the circles of life.

Counting

Now that I have grown older,
I don't worry at all
About gray hairs, extra pounds,
Or little aches and pains.
I have so many of each by now
That I count my loses instead of gains.

In Time Of Sickness

Jesus, Love and Healer of Humanity,
Here is your servant, whom you love.
She is sick and troubled.
Lay your gentle, powerful hands upon her
And make her well.

Revive her spirit, Lord.
Restore her strength so that
She continues to serve You.
Give her back to her family, friends,
And all she enriches in her life.

You have told us to ask for what we want,
And it would be granted.
And so we come in faith, and boldly make our plea.
But if it is your will that she drink this cup,
Your will be done.

Then may she join her sufferings with Yours
For the redemption of the world.
Jesus, Resurrection and Life, raise her up, we pray.

To Lyle

You've been a part of me
For over fifty years.
At night, when we're apart
I lie awake and wonder
What life would be without you.

I don't want to know.

Persistence

I looked for Him, but did not find.
I read and prayed, my eyes were blind.
But all at once, He spoke my name
And calmed my fears, erased my shame.

And now I know, deep down inside
The times I hurt, the times I cried,
He walked with me every time.
The difference now, His faith is mine.

Secrets

There are things
That you can't tell anyone –
Not even your best friend.
Night things—dark things
That you must keep secret.

Because if you told,
You'd expose a gaping wound,
And a chink of vulnerability
In your armor of
Respectability.

But there is One
Who always knows,
Who knows your every thought,
Passion, desire, action, or
Lack of action.

He knows, and loves, and
Forgives.

Cleanse Me

Wash me clean, Dear Jesus.
Open my eyes,
Sharpen my senses,
Clear my mind,
Quiet my fears.

Slow me down, O Lord
So that I may listen--
Listen with an uncluttered
Mind and heart
To You, My God .

And to those others in
Whom You dwell.
That I may grow in my
Love of you and learn
Your will for me.

An Artist's Prayer

O Lord, You who made the glorious sky,
Formed the majestic mountains,
Engineered the millions of plant life
From the insignificant grass blade
To the tall, stately redwoods,
Peopled the world with frolicking birds,
Roaming animals and cavorting fish—
And no less the great diversity of humanity,
Hear my prayer.

Guide your imperfect creation, Man,
To a greater love of You.
Show us how to cease the violence,
Child abuse, crimes against ourselves
And against others, and live in peace
As individuals and as nations.
Help us strengthen the family again
So that children are nurtured and loved,
For therein lies our future.

Promises

"The promises of the Lord are sure…" Ps. 13,7

When doubts and fears assail me
From places I know not where,
I call out to my savior
And He always answers my prayer.

In the midst of trial and suffering
When I'm bowed low by care,
I remember the One who is listening
One who will always be there.

Thankfulness

I thank you Lord, for being my God.
For always was, and ever shall be.
I thank thee for this world in which you placed me
The universe so wide and mysterious,
The earth so full of surprises,
From the sandy desserts to the lush rainforests,
For the waters that gave us life and continue
To feed and refresh us.
I thank thee for others – for relationships,
For our pets, our children, mothers, fathers,
Sisters, brothers, and all.
You have given us all we would ever need.
Let us give thanks and not look for more.

What I've Learned In The Last Seventy Years

Nothing is 'fair' in this world. Otherwise, we wouldn't need a heaven.

Happiness comes from within, not from something or someone outside oneself.

You get just what you pay for.

God never forsakes you, even though you may forget about Him.

You can't be sure of your faith or your morals until they're tested.

Never stop learning or dreaming.

Be open to new ideas, but don't rush too fast to change.

Animals have emotions and can think.

Children should be allowed to take some risks, because that's how we learn.

We also learn best by doing and by teaching others.

Creativity comes from God, and everyone has it to some degree.

We can lose what we have by not using it. This applies to mind, body, and spirit.

Good is within every human being, but so is Evil.

The devil exists and is active.

There are no coincidences, but there are accidents.

God does not cause bad things to happen, but He can stop them through prayer if it is His will.

God can make good come from bad.

Nothing is ever as bad as it seems.

All things are possible through prayer.

Be prepared for the worst, but don't anticipate it.

Be careful what you pray for – things may not happen exactly as you wish.

God's time is not our time – we can't rush Him.

Good health is a blessing; thank God for it every day.

The best prayer is one of gratitude.

To do God's will, we must relinquish our own.

Words are not necessary to pray to God; simply sit in His Presence in silence and awe.

(con't.)

My greatest learning did not come from school, but from what I
learned about people and relationships.

You never know what's in a person's heart until you ask them.

Learn to listen with undivided attention and hear what's said between
the lines.

People are threatened when you move onto their turf.

Children act as if they don't want discipline, but are grateful to have it.

Adults are just grown children, especially males.

Men's sexual desire is stimulated by their hormones, women's by their
minds.

We learn by application and practice, and this is the reason why real
learning is so difficult.

Pride and ego are always the causes of friction and resentment.

If you knew the kinds of life experiences your enemy has had, he
would not be your enemy.

It never pays to prejudge anyone, because ten times out of ten, you'd
be wrong.

A pleasant smile will sometimes disarm a belligerent individual
– remember the story of Davy Crockett and the bear!

Anger hurts everyone, especially the angry one. Forgiveness is best.

Thank God if you have a bad memory—you can forget the pain and
the wrongs.

Always find something to praise in an individual before you criticize.

The positive is always better than the negative, except in art and
photography.

Time is relentless – it keeps on going, no matter what.

But yet, time has its benefits.

Give your trust to God, not to humans.

There is Divine Order in everything.

Prayers are always answered, but sometimes not in the way you'd expect.

Where there is trust, there is no doubt.

Balance is necessary for a good life: balance work with play, rest with
activity, solitude with companionship, learning with teaching,
giving with receiving.

The best prayer is one of gratitude.

God puts you just where you need to be.

It doesn't matter what you accomplish in life, only whom you become.

At The End

Will You come and take my hand
When my days on earth are o'er?
Will You help me cross the darkened land
To the far off, shining shore?

Will You ignore my sinful past
And love me as I am?
Your child, friend, and lover at last
No defenses, no excuses, no sham?

Will You calm my fears of dying
And lead me gently through
The pain, regrets and crying
As I turn from them to You?

Will You comfort those I leave behind
With some small gentle sign
That I am still with them in mind
Until it becomes their time?

The Front Porch Swing

Unpainted wood strips, chain loops and metal hangers
Make up something as mundane as a porch swing.
A nice accessory to a front porch, it invites the owners
To sit and swing as a diversion from daily routine.

But to me, it invokes memories of my childhood
Memories of summertime swinging with my mother.
In early evenings after the day was over,
We'd sit and swing and talk and listen.

My mother was a strict disciplinarian.
Raised in the Victorian era, she never hugged
Or kissed me. Her corrections were swift
And often brutal.

I would never have known I was loved as a child
If it were not our times on the swing.
She'd hold my hand and play with my fingers.
The closeness we had was complete.

She died young, a victim of overwork and worry.
I was left without her wisdom and strength
In my early teens. Had she lived,
My life might have been much different.

This symbol of love hangs on my own front porch,
A place of healing and meditation.
How strange that this simple swinging object
Still fills the emptiness in my soul.

The Pleasure Of The Senses

Children's laughter in the park,
Crickets chirping on a summer's night,
The mournful cooing of a dove,
My cat's purring as she's stroked.
Piano music in the high register,
The close harmony of a church choir.
The patter of raindrops on the skylight,
The crunch of footsteps on new snow.

Sunset over the Arkansas River,
Storm clouds with the sun peeking through.
Reds, purples, turquoise, lime on my palette,
The sparkle of diamonds, topaz, tanzanite.
My grandbaby's shiny black eyes,
And her pink, bow-shaped lips.
Deep blue skies peeking through trees,
Purple mountains rising in the distance.

Strawberries and cream,
Hot crisp French fries,
Pineapple and mango textures,
Ice cold beer on a hot summer's eve.
Ice cream rich with sugar and eggs,
Salt on a frozen margarita,
Hot, stringy cheese on a pizza,
And cool water when you're thirsty.

A cool breeze on a warm summer's day,
My husband's hand in mine.
A gentle massage of feet and toes,
And the touch of cool rain on my brow.
My cat's strong, round tail,
And the soft, supple fur on her back.
Warm sand on bare feet,
And a splash in the backyard pool.

Honeysuckle over the back yard fence,
Freshly brewed coffee in a mug.
Mowed lawns after a rain,
Lavender potpourri on the dresser top.
Roses and carnations in a vase,
Fresh popcorn at the movies.
The smell of hay in the autumn,
And bacon sizzling in the pan.

Stranger On The Shore

As we approached the shore; tired, disheveled, and cross;
I saw Him standing there motioning to us.
He shouted, "Have you caught some fish?"
We called back –"Nothing, nothing all night."
"Try the right side of the boat," He countered.
Against all hope, we did—and our nets were close
To breaking with the great amount of fish we had snared.

And then I understood, and looked again at my Savior
Who was now bending down to start a fire.
"My Lord and My God!" I breathed and jumped
Headlong into the water. I swam rapidly -
My heart pounding. I reached Him
Long before my friends in the boat.
He smiled at me and said, "Come, have some breakfast."

My Lord had cooked breakfast for me!
How humble and forgiving He was,
Even after I had abandoned Him so
Cravenly at His death.
I vowed to give Him my all— To die in His service
And to be with him for all eternity.
I love Him above all else I have ever known.

Dichotomy

The flow of ink on paper,
Whether it results in a drawing
Or in a series of sentences,
Is a linkage of the mind
And the hand—
The spiritual and the physical.

As humans, we must know
That we are both.
That our souls and our bodies
Are inextricably woven
In life-- and in death.

In death, we leave this body behind.
But do we also leave our consciousness?
Does our soul go to judgment
With no recollection of our
Lives, our loves, our follies?

Or is the mind still active—
A conscious part of the soul?
Does the physical still remain
Part of us after death?
Are we not to rise again
Both body and soul?

My Abc's Of Gratitude

A IS FOR AIR

What a blessing is the air around us without which we couldn't breathe, and the atmosphere which protects us from the damaging effects of the sun. When I think of breath, I think of God breathing life into the first man, and I realize how fortunate we are to be loved and cared for by this Creator, and by His personification, Jesus Christ. When my last breath is taken, may its exhalation transport me into Your Heavenly Kingdom, O God.

B IS FOR BEAUTY

"Beauty sustains the human heart in the midst of pain and despair."
Joan Chittister.
"For the beauty of the earth..." Many places in the Bible speak of the beauty in the world. No artist could ever compare to the supreme artist, God. Just look at how the leaves change color in the fall: the golds, yellows, oranges and reds against the dark greens of firs and pines. The clouds at sunset or sunrise are an explosion of color – pinks, purples, indigos, oranges against the rays of the lowered sun. Even common weeds and shrubs are a riot of color in the fall. And that's not all. All you have to do is look at a lily, an iris, or a butterfly to see traces of God's grandeur. Beauty lifts us above the ordinary and brings order out of chaos. It is necessary for the soul. I thank you, Lord, for the beauty of the earth.

C IS FOR COLOR

I tried to think of another 'C' that I was grateful for since I had already considered the colors of nature in the section above. I thought of courage – I have very little of that; confidence – I'm lacking in that area as well; community – my circle of friends is very small. I had to come back to color, for that is what charges me up and makes my heart sing for joy. I open my pastel box or my palette, and the bright, pure colors give me a high that has nothing to do with drugs. I want to get in there and start painting immediately. My eyes seek the bright intense colors around me in clothes, furnishing, paintings, books, and papers. But I also love the subdued harmonies of analogous color schemes that give rest to my soul. For all this, I thank you, Lord.

D IS FOR DEATH

Yes, that's right – it's death I'm grateful for. Without death, how could we appreciate life? Without death, how could we appreciate birth? Knowing that there is a cycle to living helps us realize that all things regenerate into another life – whether it is in fueling new growth in the ground, procreating a new generation, or living a life after death in the kingdom of Heaven. Without death, how could we anticipate rebirth? Why else did God become human like us – to show us that death should not be feared. It is only a portal into another more perfect creation of His.

E IS FOR ENDURANCE

The gift of endurance is mine, and for this I am grateful. I have outlasted crises major and minor, and all these have passed. Nothing is ever as bad as we think it will be. I know that I will have many more trials to endure before my life is ended, but I trust that God will give me the grace and strength to endure them. I have not been tested enough as yet, I know, and the worst is yet to come, but I will survive it—I pray to the Holy Spirit for His blessed assurance – My soul rests in God alone, from whom comes my salvation." Psalm 62.

F IS FOR FORGIVENESS

Where would we be without God's forgiveness? Surely, this is one of the greatest gifts we've been given. All we have to do is ask for it. But what about us? The Lord's Prayer says: "Forgive us our trespasses as we forgive those who trespass against us." A tall order—for some, forgiving takes a long time, and for some, it never happens. When someone is hurt so deeply, she can turn this hurt into anger, vengeance, or hatred so easily without the help of God. Being angry or hurt does not get a person anywhere. Forgiveness strengthens the forgiver. So we must pray to be able to forgive, and forgiveness will come. And then we truly can be one of God's children again. Remind me, Lord, over and over of the need for forgiveness.

G IS FOR GOD WITH US

By this I mean that God is with, within, among, beside, in front of, behind, under, over, everywhere. There is no place He is without, regardless of the evil and suffering in the world. We must look for Him in each other, in ourselves, in Holy Scripture, and most importantly, in the events of our daily life. How do we know that God is not acting when he sends friends to us when we need them most – when we are grieving, or lonely, or upset? How do we know God is not acting when we meet a stranger down on his luck, who needs gas in his car, or carfare to work? Could this not be Jesus who needs our help?

Help me, Lord, look for your divine hand in all that occurs today – in all I do and what happens around me. Help me to see the face of Jesus in all I come in contact with today, and above all, help me recognize Your Presence in myself.

H IS FOR HOPE

O God, I thank you for the gift of hope. Hope is the belief that things will be better – that good will come eventually out of any bad or difficult situation. As Judith of Norwich said, "And all will be well, all will be well." My favorite phrase from an unknown source is, "This too, shall pass." And it is true. The storm always passes, and in the midst of its destruction, the sky clears, the birds sing, life again appears, and people rebuild. The grandest hope of all is the hope of resurrection. I believe your promises, Lord, and I hope to see them fulfilled.

I IS FOR IMAGINATION

Imagination could be a blessing or a curse. It is a blessing when it is used constructively, as in inventing, composing, painting, teaching, etc. But it is a curse if it is used to conjure up fears, evil intentions, or destructive mechanisms. Imagination has to be nurtured and encouraged. It can be squelched easily. Young children possess it, but can lose it as they grow older and experience the cares of society and peer pressure. It is not the same as creativity; creativity implies a process and a product. Imagination give us the "what if." It can lead us to a higher communion with God and a more perfect prayer life.

J IS FOR JESUS

Thank you, God, for being Jesus—not just because you died for our sins, but chiefly because you become one of us—you lived with us, drank with us, ate with us, prayed with us, cried with us, and laughed with us. You helped us understand your great love for us—undeserved and unconditional. I think of Jesus as the big brother I never had, but even more as someone who loves me unconditionally. This is hard to comprehend because I think of myself so often as unlovable. If we only knew the great love God has for us – why can I not accept this? He sent us Jesus—Jesus—Jesus—the name above all others.

K IS FOR KINDNESS

I thank God for the kindness of others – not for the kindness I show, because I'm still learning how to be kind to others. Mercy is not one of my spiritual gifts, but I'm working on it, Lord. People around me have been kind to me—they've supported me in all kinds of endeavors, complimented me where deserved, and admonished me when needed. I have often received little thank-you notes for something I've done, and I have started sending thank-you notes to others for their kindness. I have also started speaking to strangers, and complimenting others when I can. This is the meaning of Jesus words: "Do as you would be done by." Give me compassion, Lord.

L IS FOR LAUGHTER

Laughter is something I don't get enough of, but something that is greatly appreciated, especially in other people. I love to hear a child's laughter – a real "belly laugh!" Kids can laugh when something is not even funny. One of our sons is like that – he laughs all the time, and so does my son-in-law. How much better to be like that than to be so serious all the time. I give myself permission to have fun. Praise God for comedians, funny books, jokes, plays and movies that are comedies, games, and all expressions of light-heartedness. Praise God for the sound of laughter, for giggles, for snickers, and "hee-haws!"

M IS FOR MUSIC

I am so grateful for the gift of music, especially the majestic, soaring, rich sounds of a full orchestra playing the compositions of Resphigi, Tchaikovsky, Mahler, or Puccini. I marvel at mere man, that he can put together such textures, harmonies, and timbres. God had to inspire them. I feel the same way about playing the organ – so many different sounds to produce such praises to God – from quiet, restful hymns to glorious, all the stops out works with trumpets and woodwinds. The full emotions of man are exposed in music, and God has given us this power.

N IS FOR NEWNESS

See poem: Ode to Newness, p.44

O IS FOR OPENESS

Honest, candid, and genuine—I respect and am grateful for friends and family who are open. You know what to expect from them; there are no surprises or mysteries. They are who they are with no pretense. I hope to be like this as well with my family, friends, and acquaintances. I want to say what I mean, and mean what I say, but tactfully and with compassion. However, I know that my natural reticence keeps me from being more open to others. I tend to withdraw from many social situations because of timidity. Help me grow, O Lord.

P IS FOR PATIENCE

Yes, I have grown in patience over the years. From raising eight children, one of which was profoundly retarded, to teaching for over 16 years in a public high school, to serving as vice-principal in that same high school, to working for state government after that; I have learned patience and am grateful for that learning. Patience has a lot to do with "letting go and letting God," especially since we cannot see the whole picture. If one understands the limits of personal control and is able to turn one's will over to God, he/she can learn patience too. Patience keeps us sane in the midst of troubles and leads to inner peace. The trick is to know when to have patience, and when to insist on a change of situation or attitude. This is better known as wisdom.

Q IS FOR QUESTIONING

I have been questioning most of my life. My mother often punished me for this. She couldn't understand that my "whys" were legitimate and important to me. Every two-year old begins the questioning cycle which peaks during the adolescent years. This is an important part of learning and growing. If one does not question tradition, authority, the "status quo" at some time in one's life, he/she will become rigid in thinking, overly conservative, and prone to accept changes and other people's viewpoints and beliefs. The universality of the question, "Why," leads to science, theology, history, art, literature, and math. It is akin to curiosity, without which a people become stagnant and mundane.

R IS FOR ROUTINE

I love Mondays, because it means I can get back into a routine – working on a timeline, a schedule, and certain projects. It's nice to take a vacation – to get away from the usual and relax, but how great it is to return again. Knowing what to do and when to do it takes a lot of tension out of your day! Can you imagine what it would be like to have nothing to do, no place to go, no one to see, and no duty to perform? Work is a pleasure to me. Order is paramount.

S IS FOR SOLITUDE

It is not easy to find solitude in the activities and foibles of daily life. But find it I must, because I crave it. I like having people around me, but there must be some part of my day when I am alone. Maybe some of this is because I am an artist, and this is a solitary endeavor. One cannot talk to God when there are people and noise around. Silence is a requirement for solitude. Both are necessary for prayer. I have a place that I go every morning to pray and read scripture. I should spend more time there, but I haven't grown enough for that as yet. Contemplation and meditation are forms of prayer that bring one closer to the presence of God than any other method. It is necessary to still the mind and body, listen, and let go of distractions to pray in this manner. Please, God, help me find the solitude that I need to be in communion with You.

T IS FOR TIME

I thank God for time – for having lived long enough to see my children and some of my grandchildren grown – to have a comfortable life with no financial burdens – to have the companionship of my husband for so long. But most of all, I thank God for giving me the time to develop a deeper relationship with Him, to appreciate his love and mercy, to understand His promises, and to strive to do His will.

Time is relative: at times, it seems too long, at others, it is much too short, especially for those of us who are so active. It is an artificial concept; it has no meaning. It will collapse on itself at the end. Only God is everlasting.

U IS FOR USEFULLNESS

There are many ways I can be of service to others – God has given me talents and abilities which I have developed. I have been trained as an educator, and given many opportunities to expand my knowledge and understanding. I have used these gifts in Stephen Ministry, as a Prison Mentor, as a workshop leader, and am now serving as an advocate for the Marriage Tribunal in my diocese. I sing in the choir and am a

101

substitute organist. I teach art classes, volunteer at local schools, and teach my grandchildren music. I am also useful to my own children in many ways. I pray that I may continue to be useful as long as I am physically and mentally able. What good is being blessed by God if you don't spread that blessing to others?

V IS FOR VARIETY

What a paradox! Even though I love routine, I also love variety. "Variety is the spice of life," it has been said, and I'm a prime example. Psalm 104 is one of my favorite psalms because it encompasses all of creation: "How varied are your works, Lord! In wisdom you have wrought them all, the earth is full of your creatures." I have always been more of a generalist than a specialist: I draw and paint, teach, write poetry and essays, play the piano and organ, sing in the choir, and love to dance. I am always busy because I have so many various activities, but I love doing these things. All I ask is that the Lord keep me from overdoing – I tend to go off in too many directions at the same time! Sometimes I need to slow down and meditate. Help me with this, O Lord.

W IS FOR WISDOM

People automatically think a person possesses wisdom when they are elderly. Perhaps this is right, but wisdom can also be had by the very young. My wisdom was a long time in coming. Long years of experience contributed to this. I pray for the kind of wisdom that lets me differentiate between good and evil, helps me to discern the workings of the Holy Spirit in my life, and assists me in making right decisions. I look for the kind of wisdom that keeps me from making snap judgments of people and situations. I understand clearly that there are some things that I cannot control, and I must rely on the wisdom of the Lord to guide me.

X IS FOR THE UNKNOWN QUANTITY

X is sometimes used as a symbol for Christ, as well as for the unknown quantity in algebra. There is no way that I can understand the vastness of the universe, quantum physics, or the unified field theory. I can't understand how God could have existed from all time. There is no point in worrying about any of these things; I just have to accept them. I have no idea what is going to happen to me and my family in the future. But not knowing is a blessing. The best way for me is the simple way – trusting in the Lord Jesus and believing His promises.

Y IS FOR YEARNING

"O God, you are my God—for you I long! For you my body yearns; for you my soul thirsts like a land parched lifeless, and without water." Psalm 63. How well the psalms express the yearning that every creature feels for God. Some believe that there is a "God Gene" – a part of our makeup that God imbued with a longing for communion with Him. We are all spiritual in some way or another; we are not whole until we have satisfied this longing. I will never be satisfied until I can unite my mind, body and spirit to the Divine. "As the deer longs for streams of water so my soul longs for you, O God." Ps. 42

Z IS FOR ZEAL

As St. Benedict writes, "Just as there is an evil zeal of bitterness which separates us from God and leads to hell, so there is a good zeal which separates us from vices and leads to God and life everlasting." I applaud the zeal of believers such as Mother Teresa, who willingly give up everything to help the unfortunate and the poor, and I deplore the zeal of those believers who kill innocent people in the name of their God. I pray for the good zeal so that I can follow God's command to minister to those in need, even if it means sacrificing my time, treasure, and talent. Give me the fire of your love, O Lord, as you did to those disciples on Pentecost.

I Wrote A Poem

I wrote a poem
And it was good;
The rhyme and rhythm
Was as it should.

It came to me
As in sleep I dreamt--
A poem of joy
Was what it meant.

But on awakening,
The poem had fled.
The very first line
Was all I had.

As far the rest,
I have no clue.
And so, I guess
This will have to do.

Printed in the United States
99788LV00002B/1-99/A